Italian for

Beginners

• The COMPLETE Crash Course to
Speaking Italian in 5 DAYS OR LESS! •

By Bruno Thomas & Gianni Nucci

Table of Contents

INTRODUCTION

This ebook is a basic guide to the Italian language. The main goal is to inform readers about the most important grammar rules and common phrases of the Italian language.

"Italian for Beginners" doesn't offer an exhaustive grammar and vocabulary; however it is very useful if you are a beginner and if you want to travel to Italy.

* The vocabulary inside the guide is presented in the following format:

Word in English • Word in Italian • Phonetic Spelling • IPA (International Phonetic Alfabeth)

IPA and Our Special Phonetic Spelling

IPA symbols can be confusing when learning a foreign language. This is because some of them don't look like the letters of our common alphabet. For examples: ø, ɛ, ɥ, ɔ̃.

Why don't we just use our usual letters, you ask? Since this guide is for English speakers learning Italian, the following explanations apply only to English and Italian:

a) Written letters can be pronounced in different ways, depending on various factors. For example, lead (the metal) versus lead (the infinitive verb), can versus can't and led (past tense of lead) versus lead (the metal).

b) Some sounds quite simply don't exist in English words, e.g. the Italian R. Or, in reverse, some English sounds don't exist in Italian, such as the "h" in "hotel".

For these reasons, among many others, an international alphabet has been set up to cover all 'sounds' in all languages.

We will, however, try to give you the Italian pronunciation using regular letters of the alphabet, in case you don't know how to read IPA. We have called this PS, which stands for "phonetic spelling".

It is also for the reasons above that some Italian sounds are impossible to 'write' in PS, because English-speakers simply don't know how to shape their mouths to pronounce these sounds. Trying to write it in PS leads to a very strange series of letters, as you will discover!

The PS we have listed in this guide, therefore, is just a guide and will not enable you to pronounce Italian perfectly. Nevertheless, it is the best representation of how an English-speaker, who doesn't understand IPA, will be able to pronounce an Italian word.

It isn't perfect, but it's as close as you're going to get without the IPA and will certainly enable you to be understood by an Italian speaker. With time, as you begin hearing Italian spoken by natives, experience will iron out the roughness of your accent and give your Italian more finesse.

On that note, here are some explanations on the PS in this guide.

Italian Vowels and Phonetic Spelling

Vowels in Italian are very important. Every single syllable and most Italian words end with a vowel, so pronouncing them correctly is key to expressing exactly what you need to say.

- A

In Italian, the letter A is always pronounced in the same way as the A in the English word "machine", with no exceptions. For this reason, you will find the word machine translated as:

Machine • macchina • mak-kee-na• 'makkina

When the stress in a word is on the vowel A, this A should be pronounced for slightly longer, similar to the English "Ah". In the word "macchina", the stress is on the first syllable (PS: "mak"); therefore, you should pronounce this A for slightly longer as compared to the A of the English "machine".

- E

The vowel "e" can be stressed both è and é. The difference lies only in the pronunciation. The first è is pronounced with an open mouth (like the E in the English word "text"), instead of é, which is pronounced with a more closed mouth (like the E in the English word "declaration"):

Coffee • caffè • kaf-<u>feh</u> • kaf'fɛ

Why • perché • per-<u>ke</u> • per'ke

To help you recognize when you should use an open or closed mouth, the closed E will be kept as "e" and the open E will be written as "eh" in the PS. Just as with the letter A, when a syllable ending with E is stressed, that E should pronounced for slightly longer. Note that pronouncing the letter E with an open mouth is different from stressing on it. When a syllable containing the letter E should be pronounced with an open mouth, and that syllable is also stressed, you will find the following PS representation:

Coffee • caffè • kaf-<u>feh</u> • kaf'fɛ

The "eh" suggests that you should pronounce the syllable "feh" with an open mouth, and the underline means you <u>also </u>have a stress on that syllable.

- I

The letter I is always pronounced as in the word "Italian", with no exceptions. Just as with the letter A, when a syllable ending with I is stressed, that I should pronounced for slightly longer. In the PS, the I will be represented as "ee", as shown in the following example:

gallery • galleria • gal-le-ree-a • galle'ria

In the example above, you should pronounce the letter I clearly; however, sometimes the letter I only works to soften the sound of the letters C or G. For example:

Hello • ciao • cha-o • 'tʃaʊ

Yellow • giallo • jal-lo • 'dʒallo

In this case, the PS representation will not report the I, because it should not be clearly pronounced.

- O

As with the letter E, the O can be pronounced using an open mouth (similar to the O in the English word "above") or using a closed mouth (similar to the O in the English "word"). You will not find this difference represented by any accent in Italian. To help you recognize where you should use an open or closed mouth, the PS will show 'o' when you are supposed to use a closed mouth. When the O must be pronounced using an open mouth, you will find it represented as "oh", as in the following example:

Car • automobile • a-oo-to-<u>moh</u>-bee-le •
auto'mɔbile

As with the letter E, pronouncing the letter O with
an open mouth is different from stressing on it.
However, in the example, above you should use an
open mouth when pronouncing the syllable "moh"
and this syllable should also be stressed.

• U

This vowel should always be pronounced like the
English sound "oo". Therefore, you will find it
represented as "oo" in the PS. For example:

Owl • gufo • goo-fo • 'gufo

ITALIAN PRONUNCIATION

Italian pronunciation is very regular, so, once the rules are clear, it becomes easy to pronounce each word correctly. Italian and English both share the Latin alphabet, but most of the time the sounds represented by the letters differ considerably between the two languages.

Italian is a phonetic language, meaning that it is spoken the way it is written. Although there is no strict rule, in most Italian words the accent falls on the next-to-last syllable. Of course, there are many exceptions. When words should be stressed on the last vowel, they always have a written accent over that vowel.

> City • città • cheet-<u>ta</u> • tʃit'ta

> Virtue • virtù • veer-<u>too</u> • vir'tu

Sometimes, and not that rarely, the stress might fall onto the second next-to-last syllable. To help you recognize where to put the stress, you will find the stressed syllable underlined in the PS writing, as in the following example:

> Comb • pettine • <u>pet</u>-tee-ne • 'pettine

Note that one-syllable words do not need to be pronounced for longer. There are only few exceptions to this:

Yes • Sì • <u>see</u> • si

13

No • No • <u>noh</u> • no

here • qui • <u>kwee</u> • kwi

there • lì • <u>lee</u> • 'li

Since you should pronounce these one-syllable words longer, you will find these words underlined in the PS.

The consonant C when followed by a, o, or u has a sound similar to the English "k"; when it is followed by e and i it is similar to the English "ch", as in chocolate.

G before a, o or u and before consonants has a sound like the g in goal; before e and i, it sounds like the g in gentleman. Gli is similar to ll in million, and Gn to the ny in canyon.

H is silent, not aspirated. S followed by vowels and unvoiced consonants (c, f, p, q, s, t) is pronounced like the s in sun.

The R sound is tricky because it does not really exist in the English language. To pronounce it correctly, you should roll the tip of your tongue over the front of your palate. S followed by voiced consonants (b, d, g, l, m, n, r, v) is pronounced like the s in rose. Z can be pronounced like ds in beds, or like ts in bets.

The remaining consonants not listed here are quite similar to the English sounds. Note that when you find a double consonant in an Italian word, you should stay long on that consonant, in order to pronounce it correctly.

ITALIAN GRAMMAR

NOUNS

In the Italian language, the noun is a variable part of speech. It changes with gender (masculine and feminine) and number (singular and plural). Most Italian nouns ending in -O are masculine, such as:

cat • gatto • <u>gat</u>-to • 'gatto (m.s.)

Nouns ending in -A and -TÀ are meanwhile usually feminine:

apple • <u>me</u>la • me-la • 'mela (f.s.)

happiness • felicità • fe-lee-chee-<u>ta</u> • felitʃi'ta

Masculine plural is often given using the ending -I; feminine plural is expressed with the ending -E.

cats • gatti • <u>gat</u>-tee •'gatti (m.p.)

apples • mele • <u>me</u>-le • 'mele (f.p.)

Nouns are related to the other variable parts of speech, such as articles, adjectives and pronouns.

ARTICLES

The English article "the" can be translated into Italian in different ways. It depends on the gender and the number:

Masculine singular: IL / LO

 the boy • IL ragazzo • eel ra-<u>gat</u>-tzo • il ra'gattso

 the uncle • LO zio • lo <u>dsy</u>-o • lo 'tsio

Feminine singular: LA

 the girl • LA ragazza • la ra-<u>gat</u>-tsa • la ra'gattsa

Masculine plural: I / GLI

 the nouns • i nomi • ee <u>no</u>-mee • i 'nomi

 the uncles • GLI zii • lly <u>tsy</u>-ee • ʎi 'tsii

Feminine plural: LE

 the girls • LE ragazze • le ra-<u>gat</u>-tse • le ra'gattse

The English indeterminative article "a/an" is translated in Italian in the following ways:

Masculine singular: UN/UNO

 a boy• UN ragazzo • oon ra-<u>gat</u>-tso • un ra'gattso

Feminine singular: UNA

a girl • UNA ragazza • <u>oo</u>-na ra-<u>gat</u>-tsa • 'una ra'gattsa

The English "some" is translated in Italian in this way:

Masculine plural: DEI/DEGLI

Some boys • DEI ragazzi • de-ee ra-<u>gat</u>-tsee • 'dei ra'gattsi

Feminine plural: DELLE.

Some girls • DELLE ragazza • del-le ra-<u>gat</u>-tse • 'delle ra'gattse

ADJECTIVES

Adjectives in Italian are not invariable as in English, so you will need to make the adjective agree with the noun.

New:

Masculine singular: nuovo• <u>nwoh</u>-vo • 'nwɔvo

Feminine singular: nuova• <u>nwoh</u>-va • 'nwɔva

Masculine plural: nuovi • <u>nwoh</u>-vee • 'nwɔvi

Feminine plural: nuove • <u>nwoh</u>-ve • 'nwɔve

He has a new car • Lui ha una nuova macchina • loo-i a oo-na nwoh-va mak-kee-na • 'lui a 'una 'nwɔva ´makkina

She has many old books • Lei ha molti vecchi libri • leh-y a mol-ty vek-kee lee-bri • lɛi a 'molti 'vɛkki 'libri

The Italian adjective can come before or after the noun.

A big city • una grande città • oo-na gran-de cheet-ta • 'una 'grande tʃit'ta

A small city • una città piccola • oo-na cheet-ta pik-ko-la • 'una tʃit'ta 'pikkola

POSSESSIVE ADJECTIVES
Possessive adjectives can be preceded by the determinative article.

My:

(sing.) il mio (m)/ la mia (f) • eel mee-o/ la mee-a • il 'mio/la 'mia

(plur.) i miei (m)/le mie (f) • ee myeh-ee/le mee-e • i mi'ɛi/le 'mie

Your:

(sing.) il tuo (m)/ la tua (f) • eel <u>too</u>-o/ la too-a • il 'tuo/la 'tua

(plur.) i tuoi (m)/ le tue (f) • ee <u>twoh</u>-ee/le <u>too</u>-e • i tu'ɔi/le 'tue

His/Her/Its:

(sing.) il suo (m)/ la sua (f) • eel <u>soo</u>-o/la <u>soo</u>-a • il 'suo/la 'sua

(plur.) i suoi (m)/le sue(f)• ee <u>swoh</u>-ee/le swe • i su'ɔi/le 'sue

Our:

(sing.) il nostro (m)/ la nostra (f) • eel <u>nos</u>-tro /la <u>nos</u>-tra • il 'nɔstro/la 'nɔstra

(plur.) i nostri (m)/ le nostre (f) • ee <u>nos</u>-tree/le <u>nos</u>-tre • i 'nɔstri/le 'nɔstre

Your:

(sing.) il vostro (m)/ la vostra (f) • eel <u>vos</u>-tro/la <u>vos</u>-tra • il 'vɔstro/la 'vɔstra

(plur.) i vostri (m)/ le vostre (f)• ee <u>vos</u>-tree/le <u>vos</u>-tre • i 'vɔstri/le 'vɔstre

Their:

(sing.) il loro (m)/la loro (f) • eel <u>lo</u>-ro/la <u>lo</u>-ro • il 'loro/la 'loro

(plur.) i loro (m)/le loro (f) • ee <u>lo</u>-ro/ le <u>lo</u>-ro • i 'loro/le 'loro

In English, the singular third person is referred to as the possessor, while in Italian it is referred to as the noun.

The English second person of the possessive adjective "your" is the same for singular and plural, but in Italian it changes: "tuo/tua/tuoi/tue" for the singular second person of the possessive adjective and "vostro/ vostra/ vostri/ vostre" for the plural one.

Italian possessive pronouns are like possessive adjectives and follow the same rules.

PERSONAL PRONOUNS

Italian personal pronouns can be omitted in phrases.

I • io • <u>ee</u>-o • 'io

You • tu • too • tu

He • egli/lui • <u>e</u>-lly/<u>loo</u>-ee • 'eʎʎi/'lui

She • ella/lei • <u>el</u>-la/<u>leh</u>-ee • 'ella/lɛi

It • esso /essa • <u>es</u>-so/<u>es</u>-sa • 'esso/'essa

21

We • noi • <u>no</u>-ee • noi

You • voi • <u>vo</u>-ee • voi

They • essi/loro • <u>es</u>-see/<u>lo</u>-ro • 'essi/'loro

The third person forms (m)"egli", "esso" (pl. "essi") and (f)"ella", "essa" (pl. "esse") are used in the written language only; "egli" and "ella" denotes only persons, while "esso" and "essa" (pl. "essi", "esse") refer to both persons and things.

However, the distinction of the neuter gender does not cause any important change because all other parts of the sentence (nouns, verb inflections, adjectives etc.) do not have a neuter gender, which is simply handled by using either masculine or feminine.

VERBS

Romance languages such as Italian have separate forms of address in formal versus informal situations. There are four ways of saying "you" in Italian: Tu (singular) and voi (plural) are the familiar forms, only used with family members, children, and friends. Lei (for one person, male or female) and its plural Loro are used in more formal situations to address strangers, older people or those in authority.

May we switch to the tu form? • Possiamo darci del tu? • Pos-sya-mo dar-chee del too • possi'amo 'dartʃi del tu

Verbs after "Lei" are conjugated like a 3rd person singular.

You are a grandmother • Lei è nonna • leh-ee eh nohn-na • lɛi ɛ 'nɔnna

SIMPLE PRESENT – TO BE
to be • essere • ehs-se-re • ' ɛssere

I am • io sono • ee-o so-no • 'io 'sono

You are • tu sei • too seh-ee • tu sɛi

He/ She/ It is • (m) Egli/ (f) Ella è • e-lly / el-la eh • 'eʎʎi / 'ella ɛ

We are • noi siamo • no-ee sya-mo • noi si'amo

You are • voi siete • vo-ee sye-te • voi sjɛte

They are • essi sono • es-see so-no • 'essi 'sono

SIMPLE PRESENT – TO HAVE
to have • avere • a-ve-re • a'vere

I have got • io ho • ee-o oh • 'io 'ɔ
23

You have got • tu hai • too <u>a</u>-ee • tu ai

He / She / It has got • Egli/ Ella ha • <u>e</u>-lly / <u>el</u>-la a • 'eʎʎi / 'ella a

We have got • noi abbiamo • <u>no</u>-ee ab-<u>bya</u>-mo • noi ab'bjamo

You have got • voi avete • <u>vo</u>-ee a-<u>ve</u>-te • voi a'vete

They have got • essi hanno • <u>es</u>-see <u>an</u>-no • 'essi 'anno

SIMPLE PRESENT – VERBS ENDING IN -ARE
To think • pensARE • pen-sa-re • pen'sare

I think • io penso • <u>ee</u>o <u>pen</u>-so • io 'penso

You think • tu pensi • too <u>pen</u>-see • tu 'pensi

He/ she/ it thinks • egli/ ella pensa • <u>e</u>-lly / <u>el</u>-la <u>pen</u>-sa • 'eʎʎi / 'ella 'pensa

We think • noi pensiamo • <u>no</u>-ee pen-<u>sya</u>-mo • noi pen'sjamo

You think • voi pensate • <u>vo</u>-ee pen-<u>sa</u>-te • voi pen'sate

They think • essi pensano • <u>es</u>-see <u>pen</u>-sa-no • 'essi 'pensano

VERBS ENDING IN –ERE

To answer • rispondERE • ris-pon-de-re • ris'pondere

I answer • io rispondo • <u>ee</u>-o rees-<u>pon</u>-do • 'io ris'pondo

You answer • tu rispondi • too rees-<u>pon</u>-dee • tu ris'pondi

He/ She/ It answers • egli/ ella risponde • <u>e</u>-lly / <u>el</u>-la rees-<u>pon</u>-de • ' eʎʎi / 'ella ris'ponde

We answer • noi rispondiamo • <u>no</u>-ee rees-pon-<u>dya</u>-mo • noi rispon'djamo

You answer • voi rispondete • <u>vo</u>-ee ris-pon-<u>de</u>-te • voi rispon'dete

They answer • essi rispondono • <u>es</u>-see rees-<u>pon</u>-do-no • essi ris'pondono

VERBS ENDING IN –IRE

To sleep • dormIRE • dor-<u>mee</u>-re • dor'mire

I sleep • io dormo • <u>ee</u>-o <u>dor</u>-mo • 'io 'dormo

You sleep • tu dormi • too <u>dor</u>-mee • tu 'dormi

He/ She/ It sleeps • egli/ ella dorme • <u>e</u>-lly / <u>el</u>-la <u>dor</u>-me • ' eʎʎi / 'ella 'dorme

We sleep • noi dormiamo • <u>no</u>-ee dor-<u>mya</u>-mo • noi dor'mjamo

You sleep • voi dormite • vo-ee dor-mee-te • voi dor'mite

They sleep • essi dormono • es-see dor-mo-no • essi 'dormono

NUMBERS, DAYS, MONTHS & SEASONS

What day is it today? • Che giorno è oggi? • ke jor-no eh ohd-djee • ke 'dʒorno ɛ 'ɔddʒi

It's the 18th of May • E' il 18 Maggio • eh eel dee-choht-to mad-djo • ɛ il di'tʃɔtto 'maddʒo

NUMBERS

CARDINAL NUMBERS (All these numbers are m.s.)

0 • zero • dzeh-ro • ' dzɛro

1 • uno • oo-no • 'uno

2 • due • doo-e • 'due

3 • tre • tre • tre

4 • quattro • kwat-tro • 'kwattro

5 • cinque • cheen-que • 'tʃinkwe

6 • sei • seh-ee • 'sɛi

7 • sette • <u>seht</u>-te • 'sɛtte

8 • otto • <u>oht</u>-to • 'ɔtto

9 • nove • <u>noh</u>-ve • 'nɔve

10 • dieci • <u>dyeh</u>-chee • 'djɛtʃi

11 • undici • <u>oon</u>-dee-chee • 'unditʃi

12 • dodici • <u>do</u>-dee-chee • 'doditʃi

13 • tredici • <u>tre</u>-dee-chee • 'treditʃi

14 • quattordici • <u>kwat</u>-tor-dee-chee • kwat'torditʃi

15 • quindici • <u>kween</u>-dee-chee • 'kwinditʃi

16 • sedici • <u>se</u>-dee-chee • 'seditʃi

17 • diciassette • dee-chas-<u>seht</u>-te • /ditʃas'sɛtte

18 • diciotto • dee-<u>choht</u>-to • di'tʃɔtto

19 • diciannove • dee-chan-<u>noh</u>-ve • ditʃan'nɔve

20 • venti • <u>ven</u>-tee • 'venti

21 • ventuno • ven-<u>too</u>-no • ven'tuno

22 • ventidue • ven-tee-<u>doo</u>-e • venti'due

30 • trenta • <u>tren</u>-ta • 'trenta

40 • quaranta • kwa-<u>ran</u>-ta • kwa'ranta

50 • cinquanta • cheen-<u>kwa</u>-nta • tʃin'kwanta

60 • sessanta • ses-<u>san</u>-ta • ses'santa

70 • settanta • set-<u>tan</u>-ta • set'tanta

80 • ottanta • ot-<u>tan</u>-ta • ot'tanta

90 • novanta • no-<u>van</u>-ta • no'vanta

100 • cento • <u>chen</u>-to • 'tʃɛnto

101 • centouno • chen-to-<u>oo</u>-no • tʃɛnto 'uno

200 • duecento • doo-e-<u>chen</u>-to • due' tʃɛnto

1000 • mille • <u>meel</u>-le • 'mille

one million • un milione • un mee-<u>lyo</u>-ne • un mi'ljone

ORDINAL NUMBERS (all these numbers are m.s.)

1st • primo • <u>pree</u>-mo • 'primo

2nd • secondo • se-<u>kon</u>-do • se'kondo

3rd • terzo • <u>tehr</u>-tso • 'tɛrtso

4th • quarto • <u>kwar</u>-to • 'kwarto

5th • quinto • <u>kween</u>-to • 'kwinto

6th • sesto • <u>sehs</u>-to • 'sɛsto

7th • settimo • <u>seht</u>-tee-mo • 'sɛttimo

8th • ottavo • ot-<u>ta</u>-vo • ot'tavo

9th • nono • <u>noh</u>-no • 'nɔno

10th • decimo • <u>de</u>-chee-mo • 'dɛtʃimo

11th • undicesimo • oon-dee-<u>che</u>-zee-mo • undi'tʃɛzimo

12th • dodicesimo • do-dee-<u>che</u>-zee-mo • dodi'tʃɛzimo

13th• tredicesimo • tre-dee-<u>che</u>-zee-mo • tredi'tʃɛzimo

20th• ventesimo • ven-<u>teh</u>-zee-mo • ven'tɛzimo

100th • centesimo • chen-<u>teh</u>-zee-mo • tʃen'tɛzimo

101st • centunesimo • chen-too-<u>neh</u>-zee-mo •
tʃentu'nɛzimo

102nd • centoduesimo • chen-to-doo-<u>eh</u>-zee-mo •
tʃentodu'ɛzimo

110th • centodecimo •chen-to-<u>deh</u>-chee-mo •
tʃɛnto'dɛtʃimo

200th • duecentesimo • doo-e-chen-<u>teh</u>-zee-mo •
duetʃen'tɛzimo

1000th • millesimo • mil-<u>leh</u>-zee-mo • mil'lɛzimo

DAYS

WEEK

Sunday • domenica • do-<u>me</u>-nee-ka • do'menika (f.s.)

Monday • lunedì • loo-ne-<u>dee</u> • lune'di (m.s.)

Tuesday • martedì • mar-te-<u>dee</u> • marte'di (m.s.)

Wednesday • mercoledì • mer-ko-le-<u>dee</u> • merkole'di (m.s.)

Thursday • giovedì • jo-ve-<u>dee</u> • dʒove'di (m.s.)

Friday • venerdì • ve-ner-<u>dee</u> • vener'di (m.s.)

Saturday • sabato • <u>sa</u>-ba-to • 'sabato (m.s.)

MONTHS

January • Gennaio • jen-<u>na</u>-yo • dʒen'najo (m.s.)

February • Febbraio • feb-<u>bra</u>-yo • feb'brajo (m.s.)

March • Marzo • <u>mar</u>-tso • 'martso (m.s.)

April • Aprile • a-<u>pree</u>-le • a'prile (m.s.)

May • Maggio • <u>mad</u>-djo • 'maddʒo (m.s.)

June • Giugno • <u>joon</u>-nyo • 'dʒuɲɲo (m.s.)

July • Luglio • <u>loo</u>-llyo • 'luʎʎo (m.s.)

August • Agosto • a-<u>gos</u>-to • a'gosto (m.s.)

Septembre • Settembre • set-<u>tehm</u>-bre • set'tɛmbre (m.s.)

Octobre • Ottobre • ot-<u>to</u>-bre • ot'tobre (m.s.)

Novembre • Novembre • no-<u>vehm</u>-bre • no'vɛmbre (m.s.)

Decembre • Dicembre • dee-<u>chehm</u>-bre • di'tʃɛmbre (m.s.)

SEASONS

spring • primavera • pree-ma-<u>veh</u>-ra • prima'vɛra (f.s.)

summer • estate • es-<u>ta</u>-te • es'tate (f.s.)

autumn • autunno • a-oo-<u>toon</u>-no • au'tunno (m.s.)

winter • inverno • een-<u>vehr</u>-no • in'vɛrno (m.s.)

WHAT IS THE ITALIAN FOR?

MEETING PEOPLE

BASIC WORDS AND PHRASES

Hello • Ciao • tcha-o • 'tʃao

Hi • Salve • sal-ve • 'salve

Good morning • Buongiorno • bwon-jor-no • bwon'dʒorno

Good afternoon • Buon pomeriggio • bwon po-me-ryd-djo • 'bwɔn pome'riddʒo

Good evening • Buona sera • bwoh-na se-ra • 'bwɔna 'sera

Good night • Buona notte • bwoh-na noht-te • 'bwɔna 'nɔtte

Bye • Ciao • tcha-o • 'tʃao

Good bye • Arriverderci • ar-ree-ve-der-chee • arrive'dertʃi

Yes • Sì • see • si

No • No • noh • no

Please • Per favore • per fa-vo-re • per fa'vore

Excuse me • Mi scusi • mee skoo-see • mi 'skusi

Thank you • Grazie • gra<u>t</u>-tsye • 'grattsje

You're welcome • Prego • <u>preh</u>-go • 'prɛgo

Have a nice day • Buona giornata • boo-<u>oh</u>-na jor-<u>na</u>-ta• 'bwɔna dʒor'nata

(formal) - Pleased to meet you • Piacere di conoscerla • pya-<u>che</u>-re dee ko-<u>no</u>-sher-la • pja'tʃere di ko'noʃʃerla

(informal) - Pleased to meet you • Piacere di conoscerti • pya-<u>che</u>-re dee ko-<u>no</u>-sher-tee • pja'tʃere di ko'noʃʃerti

See you later • A più tardi • a py-<u>oo tar</u>-dee • a 'pju 'tardi

See you soon • A presto • a <u>prehs</u>-to • a'prɛsto

(formal) - How are you? • Come sta? • <u>ko</u>-me sta • 'kome 'sta

(informal) - How are you? • Come stai? • <u>ko</u>-me <u>sta</u>-ee • 'kome 'stai

Fine, thanks • Bene grazie • <u>beh</u>-ne <u>gra</u>t-sye • 'bɛne 'grattsje

I am ok • Sto bene • sto <u>beh</u>-ne • sto 'bɛne

I am not very well • Non mi sento bene • non mee <u>sen</u>-to <u>beh</u>-ne • non mi 'sento 'bɛne

(formal) - Do you have a light? • Ha da accendere? • a da ac-<u>chehn</u>-de-re • a da at'tʃɛndere (informal) - Do you have a light? • Hai da accendere? • <u>a</u>-ee da ac-<u>chehn</u>-de-re • 'ai da at'tʃɛndere

Really? • Davvero? • dav-<u>ve</u>-ro • dav'vero

Good luck • Buona fortuna • <u>bwoh</u>-na for-<u>too</u>-na • 'bwɔna for'tuna

May I have …? • Posso avere…? • <u>pos</u>-so a-<u>ve</u>-re • 'posso a'vere

(formal) - Can you help me? • Può aiutarmi? • <u>pwoh</u> a-yoo-<u>tar</u>-mee • 'pwo aju'tarmi

(informal) - Can you help me? • Puoi aiutarmi? • <u>pwo</u>-ee a-yoo-<u>tar</u>-mee • 'pwoi aju'tarmi

Does somebody speak English ? • Qualcuno sa parlare inglese ? • koo-al-<u>koo</u>-no sa par-<u>la</u>-re een-<u>gle</u>-se ? • kwal'kuno sa par'lare in'glese ?

What does it mean? • Cosa significa? • <u>koh</u>-sa seen-<u>ny</u>-fee-ka • 'kɔsa si'ɲɲifika

Can you repeat it ? • Puoi ripetere ? • poo-<u>oh</u>-ee ree-<u>pe</u>-te-re ? • 'pwoi ri'pɛtere ?

Would you write that down, please ? • Lo può scrivere, per piacere ? • lo poo-<u>oh skree</u>-ve-re per pee-a-<u>che</u>-re ? • lo 'pwo 'skrivere per pja'tʃere ?

What is the Italian for… ? • Come si dice in italiano … ? • ko-me see dee-che een ee-ta-lya-no • 'kome si 'ditʃe in ita'ljano

How do you say that in Italian ? • Come si dice in italiano ? • ko-me see dee-che een ee-ta-lee-a-no ? • 'kome si 'ditʃe in ita'ljano ?

I have forgotten the word for … • Ho dimenticato come si dice … • oh dee-men-tee-ka-to ko-me see dee-che … • ɔ dimenti'kato 'kome si 'ditʃe …

How is that pronounced? • Come si pronuncia ? • ko-me see pro-noon-cha ? • 'kome si pro'nuntʃa ?

Where..? • Dove…? • do-ve • 'dove

How much…? • Quanto…? • kwan-to • 'kwanto

How many…? • Quanti…? • kwan-tee • 'kwanti

How long does it take? • Quanto tempo ci vuole? • kwan-to tehm-po chee vwo-le • 'kwanto 'tɛmpo tʃi 'vwole

Who…? • Chi…? • kee • ki

Why…? • Perché…? • per-ke • per'ke

Because • perché • per-ke • per'ke

I'd like… • Vorrei…• vor-reh-y • vor'rɛj

There is/are • C'è / Ci sono • cheh / chee <u>so</u>-no • tʃe / tʃi 'sono

PRESENTATIONS

Mr • Signore • seen-<u>nyo</u>-re • siɲ'ɲore (m.s.)

Mrs • Signora • seen-<u>nyo</u>-ra • siɲ'ɲora (f.s.)

Miss • Signorina • seen-nyo-<u>ree</u>-na • siɲɲo'rina (f.s.)

(formal) - Do you speak English? • Parla inglese? • <u>par</u>-la een-<u>gle</u>-se • 'parla in'glese

(informal) - Do you speak English? • Parli inglese? • <u>par</u>-lee een-<u>gle</u>-se • 'parli in'glese

I don't understand • Non capisco • non ka-<u>pee</u>-sko • non ka'pisko

I don't speak Italian • Io non parlo italiano • <u>ee</u>-o non <u>par</u>-lo ee-ta-<u>lya</u>-no • io non 'parlo ita'ljano

(formal) - Can you speak slower? • Può parlare più lentamente? • pwoh par-<u>la</u>-re py-<u>oo</u> len-ta-<u>men</u>-te • 'pwɔ par'lare pju lenta'mente

(informal) - Can you speak slower? • Puoi parlare più lentamente? • poo-<u>oh</u>-ee par-<u>la</u>-re py-oo len-ta-<u>men</u>-te • 'pwɔee par'lare pju lenta'mente

(formal) - What's your name? • Come si chiama? • <u>ko</u>-me see <u>kya</u>-ma • 'kome si 'kjama

(informal) - What's your name? • Come ti chiami? • <u>ko</u>-me tee <u>kya</u>-mee • 'kome ti 'kjami

My name is ... • Mi chiamo ... • mee <u>kya</u>-mo • mi 'kjamo

Nice to meet you • Piacere • pya-<u>che</u>-re • pja'tʃere

(formal) - Do you live here ? • Abita qui ? • <u>a</u>-bee-ta <u>kwee</u> ? • 'abita kwi

(informal) - Do you live here ? • Abiti qui ? • <u>a</u>-bee-tee <u>kwee</u> ? • 'abiti kwi ?

(formal) - Are you on holiday? • Lei è in vacanza? • <u>leh</u>-ee eh een va-<u>kan</u>-tsa ? • lɛi ɛ in va'kantsa ?

(informal) - Are you on holiday? • Sei in vacanza? • <u>seh</u>-i in va-<u>kan</u>-tsa ? • sɛi in va'kantsa ?

I am here ... • Sono qui ... • <u>so</u>-no <u>kwee</u> • sono kwi

On holiday • in vacanza • een va-<u>kan</u>-tsa • in va'kantsa

For business • per lavoro • per la-<u>vo</u>-ro • per la'voro

With my family/ friends • con la mia famiglia/ con miei amici • kon la <u>mee</u>-a fa-<u>mee</u>-llya / kon ee <u>myeh</u>-

ee a-<u>mee</u>-chee • kon la 'mia fa'miʎʎa/ kon i mi'ɛi a'mitʃi

(formal) - Where are you from? • Da dove viene? • da <u>do</u>-ve <u>vye</u>-ne • da 'dove 'vjene

(informal) - Where are you from? • Da dove vieni? • da <u>do</u>-ve <u>vye</u>-nee • da 'dove 'vjeni

I come from ... • Vengo da ... • <u>ven</u>-go da • 'vengo da

This is ... • Questo/a è ... • <u>kwes</u>-to/a eh • 'kwesto/a ɛ

> my friend • il/la mio/a amico/a • il/la <u>mee</u>-o/a a-<u>mee</u>-ko/a • il/la 'mio/a a'miko/a

> my son • mio figlio • <u>mee</u>-o <u>fee</u>-llyo • 'mio 'fiʎʎo

> my daughter • mia figlia • <u>mee</u>-a <u>fee</u>-llya • 'mia 'fiʎʎa

> my husband • mio marito • <u>mee</u>-o ma-<u>ree</u>-to • 'mio ma'rito

> my wife • mia moglie • <u>mee</u>-a <u>mo</u>-llye • mia 'moʎʎe

(formal) - How old are you? • Quanti anni ha? • <u>kwan</u>-tee <u>an</u>-nee a • 'kwanti 'anni a

(informal) - How old are you? • Quanti anni hai? • <u>kwan</u>-tee <u>an</u>-nee a-ee • 'kwanti 'anni 'ai

I am ... years old • Ho ... anni • o ... <u>an</u>-nee • ɔ ... 'anni (formal) - What's your occupation? • Che lavoro fa? • ke la-<u>vo</u>-ro fa• ke la'voro fa

(informal) - What's your occupation? • Che lavoro fai? • ke la-<u>vo</u>-ro <u>fa</u>-ee • ke la'voro 'fai

I am a ... • Sono un/a • so-no un/a • 'sono un/a

    student • studente • stoo-<u>dehn</u>-te • stu'dɛnte (m.s.)

    teacher • insegnante • een-sen-<u>nyan</u>-te • inseɲ'ɲante (m.s. and f.s.)

    worker • operaio • o-pe-<u>ra</u>-yo • ope'rajo (m.s.)

    housewife • casalinga • ka-sa-<u>leen</u>-ga • kasa'linga (f.s.)

    unemployed • disoccupato • dee-sok-koo-<u>pa</u>-to • dizokku'pato (m.s.)

(formal) - Are you married? • è sposato • eh spo-<u>za</u>-to • ɛ spo'zato

(informal) - Are you married? • Sei sposato • <u>seh</u>-ee spo-<u>za</u>-to • sɛi spo'zato

Do you have a boyfriend / girlfriend? • Hai un ragazzo / una ragazza ? • <u>a</u>-ee oon ra-<u>ga</u>-ttso / <u>u</u>-na ra-<u>gat</u>-tsa ? • ai un ra'gattso /una ra'gattsa ?

I am single • sono single • <u>so</u>-no <u>seen</u>-gol • 'sono 'singol married • sposato/a • spo-<u>za</u>-to/a • spo'zato

divorced • divorziato/a • dee-vor-<u>tsya</u>-to/a • divor'tsjato

widowed • vedovo/a • <u>ve</u>-do-vo/a • vedovo/a

FREE TIME

(formal) - Do you like ...? • Le piace ...? • le <u>pya</u>-che • le 'pjatʃe

(informal) - Do you like ...? • Ti piace ...? • tee <u>pya</u>-che • ti 'pjatʃe

I like/don't like ... • Mi piace/ Non mi piace ... • mee <u>pya</u>-tche / non mee <u>pya</u>-che • mi 'pjatʃe / non mi 'pjatʃe

Shopping • fare shopping • <u>fa</u>-re <u>shop</u>-peeng • 'fare 'ʃɔpping

Cooking • cucinare • koo-chee-<u>na</u>-re • kutʃi'nare

Playing • giocare • jo-<u>ka</u>-re • dʒo'kare

Dancing • ballare • bal-<u>la</u>-re • 'ballare

Singing • cantare • kan-<u>ta</u>-re • 'kantare

Listening to music • Ascoltare musica • as-kol-<u>ta</u>-re la <u>moo</u>-see-ka • askol'tare la 'musika (formal) - What do you do in your free time? • Cosa fa nel tempo libero? • <u>koh</u>-sa fa nel <u>tehm</u>-po <u>lee</u>-be-ro • 'kɔsa fa nel 'tɛmpo 'libero

(informal) - What do you do in your free time? • Cosa fai nel tempo libero? • <u>koh</u>-sa <u>fa</u>-ee nel <u>tehm</u>-po <u>lee</u>-be-ro • 'kɔsa 'fai nel 'tɛmpo 'libero

DATING

(formal) - What are you doing this evening? • Cosa fa stasera? • <u>koh</u>-sa fa sta-<u>se</u>-ra • 'kɔsa fa sta'sera

(informal) - What are you doing this evening? • Cosa fai stasera? • <u>koh</u>-sa <u>fa</u>-ee sta-<u>se</u>-ra • 'kɔsa 'fai sta'sera

(formal) - Would you like to go …? • Vorrebbe andare a …? • vor-<u>reb</u>-be an-<u>da</u>-re a • vor'rebbe an'dare a

(informal) - Would you like to go …? • Vorresti andare a …? • vor-<u>res</u>-tee an-<u>da</u>-re a • vor'resti an'dare a

Yes, I'd like to • Sì, mi piacerebbe • <u>see</u>, mee pya-che-<u>reb</u>-be • si, mi pjatʃe'rebbe

No, thanks • No, grazie • <u>noh,</u> <u>grat</u>-tsye • no 'grattsje

(formal) - Do you know a good restaurant? • Conosce un buon ristorante? • ko-<u>no</u>-she oon bwohn rees-to-<u>ran</u>-te • ko'noʃʃe un 'bwɔn risto'rante (informal) - Do you know a good restaurant? • Conosci un buon ristorante? • ko-<u>no</u>-shee oon bwohn rees-to-<u>ran</u>-te • ko'noʃʃi un 'bwɔn risto'rante

Where shall we go? • Dove andiamo? • <u>do</u>-ve an-<u>dya</u>-mo • 'dove an'djamo

Where will we meet? • Dove ci incontramo? • <u>do</u>-ve chee een-kon-<u>trya</u>-mo • 'dove tʃi inkon'trjamo

What time will we meet? • A che ora ci incontriamo? • a ke <u>o</u>-ra chee een-kon-<u>trya</u>-mo • a ke 'ora tʃi inkon'trjamo

(formal) - Do you want to come with us? • Vuole venire con noi? • <u>vwo</u>-le ve-<u>nee</u>-re kon noi • vwole ve'nire kon 'noi

(informal) - Do you want to come with us? • Vuoi venire con noi? • <u>vwo</u>-ee ve-<u>nee</u>-re kon noi • vwoi ve'nire kon 'noi

Let's meet at ... • Incontriamoci a ... • een-kon-<u>trya</u>-mo-chee a • inkon'trjamotʃi a

I'm looking forward to it • Non vedo l'ora • non <u>ve</u>-do <u>lo</u>-ra • non 'vedo 'lora

VISITING THE CITY

DIRECTIONS

(formal) - Excuse me, can you tell me where *Fontana di Trevi* is ? • Mi scusi, mi può dire dov'è la *Fontana di Trevi* ? • Mee <u>skoo</u>-see mee poo-<u>oh</u> <u>dee</u>-re do-<u>veh</u> la fon-<u>ta</u>-na dee

<u>treh</u>-vee • Mi 'skusi mi pwɔ dire do'vɛ la fon'tana di trɛvi ?

(informal) - Excuse me, can you tell me where *Fontana di Trevi* is ? • Scusami, mi può dire dov'è la *Fontana di Trevi* ? • <u>skoo</u>-sa-mee mee poo-<u>oh</u>-ee <u>dee</u>-re do-<u>veh</u> la fon-<u>ta</u>-na dee <u>tre</u>-vee • skusami mi pwoi dire do'vɛ la fon'tana di trɛvi ?

Where is the museum? • Dov'è il museo? • do-<u>veh</u> eel moo-<u>zeh</u>-o • do'vɛ il mu'zɛo

How can I get there? • Come ci si arriva? • <u>ko</u>-me chee see ar-<u>ree</u>-va • 'kome tʃi si ar'riva

How far is it? • Quanto dista? • <u>kwan</u>-to <u>dees</u>-ta • 'kwanto 'dista

How long does it take on foot ? • Quanto tempo ci vuole a piedi ? • <u>kwan</u>-to <u>tehm</u>-po chee voo-<u>oh</u>-le a pee-<u>eh</u>-dee ? • 'kwanto 'tɛmpo tʃi vwɔle a 'pjɛdi ?

It takes about fifteen minutes • Ci vogliono circa quindici minuti • chee <u>voh</u>-llyo-no <u>cheer</u>-ka <u>kween</u>-dee-chee mee-<u>noo</u>-tee • tʃi 'vɔʎʎono 'tʃirka 'kwinditʃi mi'nuti

What's the address? • Qual è l'indirizzo? • kwa-<u>leh</u> leen-dee-<u>reet</u>-tso • kwa'lɛ lindi'rittzo

(formal) - Turn left/right • Giri a sinistra/destra • <u>gee</u>-ree a see-<u>nees</u>-tra / <u>dehs</u>-tra • 'dʒiri a sinistra / 'dɛstra

(informal) - Turn left/right • Gira a sinistra/destra • <u>gee</u>-ra a see-<u>nees</u>-tra / <u>dehs</u>-tra • 'dʒira a sinistra / 'dɛstra

(formal) - Turn at the corner • Giri all'angolo • <u>gee</u>-ree al-<u>lan</u>-go-lo • 'dʒiri al'langolo

(informal) - Turn at the corner • Gira all'angolo • <u>gee</u>-ra al-<u>lan</u>-go-lo • 'dʒira al'langolo

Far • lontano • lon-<u>ta</u>-no • lon'tano

Near • vicino • vee-<u>chee</u>-no • vi'tʃino

In front of • davanti • da-<u>van</u>-tee • da'vanti

Behind • dietro • <u>dyeh</u>-tro • 'djɛtro

Straight on • dritto • <u>dreet</u>-to • 'dritto

By train • in treno • een <u>treh</u>-no • in 'trɛno

By car • in macchina • een mak-<u>kee</u>-na • in 'makkina

By bus • in autobus • een <u>a</u>-oo-to-boos • in 'autobus

On foot •A piedi • a <u>pyeh</u>-dee • a 'pjɛdi

Where are the toilets? • Dove sono i servizi igienici? • <u>do</u>-ve <u>so</u>-no ee ser-<u>veet</u>-tsee ee-<u>jeh</u>-nee-tchee • 'dove 'sono i ser'vittsi i'dʒɛnitʃi

Are there are any public toilets nearby please ? • Ci sono dei bagni pubblici nelle vicinanze per favore ? • chee <u>so</u>-no de-ee <u>ban</u>-ny <u>poob</u>-blee-chee <u>nel</u>-le vee-tchee-<u>nan</u>-tse per fa-<u>vo</u>-re ? • tʃi sono dei 'baɲɲi 'pubblitʃi 'nelle vitʃi'nantse per fa'vore ?

Where is the nearest ...? • Dov'è ... più vicino? • do-<u>veh</u> ... py-<u>oo</u> vee-<u>tchee</u>-no • do'vɛ ... pju vi'tʃino

ACCOMODATION

Where can I find a ...? • Dove posso trovare un/a ...? • <u>do</u>-ve <u>pos</u>-so tro-<u>va</u>-re un/a • 'dove 'posso tro'vare un/a

Hotel • albergo • al-<u>behr</u>-go • al'bɛrgo (m.s.)

Room • camera • <u>ka</u>-me-ra • 'kamera (f.s.)

Bed & Breakfast • bed & breakfast • bed ehnd <u>brek</u>-fast • bed ənd brekfəst (m.s.)

I'd like to book ... • vorrei prenotare ... • vor-<u>reh</u>-ee pre-no-<u>ta</u>-re • vor'rɛj preno'tare

I have got a reservation • Ho una prenotazione • oh <u>oo</u>-na pre-no-ta-<u>tsyo</u>-ne • ɔ 'una prenotat'tsjone

From ... to ... • Da ... a ... • da ... a • da a

Do you have a room? • Avete una camera? • a-<u>ve</u>-te oona <u>ka</u>-me-ra • a'vete 'una 'kamera

Single room • camera singola • <u>ka</u>-me-ra <u>seen</u>-go-la • 'kamera 'singola (f.s.)

Double room • camera matrimoniale • <u>ka</u>-me-ra ma-tree-mo-<u>nya</u>-le • 'kamera matrimo'njale (f.s.)

Twin room • camera doppia a due letti • <u>ka</u>-me-ra <u>dop</u>-pya a <u>doo</u>-e <u>leht</u>-tee • kamera doppja a due 'lɛtti (f.s.)

Can I pay by credit card? • Posso pagare con carta di credito? • <u>pos</u>-so pa-<u>ga</u>-re kon <u>kar</u>-ta dee <u>kre</u>-dee-to • 'posso pa'gare kon 'karta di 'kredito

When's lunch served? • Quando viene servito il pranzo? • <u>kwan</u>-do <u>vye</u>-ne ser-<u>vee</u>-to eel <u>pran</u>-dzo • 'kwando 'vjene ser'vito il 'prandzo

How much does it cost for …? • Quanto costa …? • <u>kwa</u>-nto <u>kos</u>-ta • 'kwanto 'kosta

One night • solo un pernottamento • <u>so</u>-lo oon per-not-ta-<u>men</u>-to • solo un pernotta'mento (m.s.)

Half board • mezza pensione • <u>med</u>-dza pen-<u>syo</u>-ne • 'mɛddza pen'sjone (f.s.)

Full board • pensione completa • pen-<u>syo</u>-ne kom-<u>pleh</u>-ta • pensjone kom'plɛta (f.s.)

May I see the room? • Posso vedere la stanza? • pos-so ve-de-re la stan-tsa • 'posso ve'dere la 'stantsa

Do you have anything cheaper? • Ne avete di più economiche? • ne a-ve-te dee pee-oo e-ko-noh-mee-ke • ne a'vete di pju eko'nɔmike

Is breakfast included? • La colazione è inclusa? • la ko-lat-tsyo-ne eh een-kloo-sa • la kolat'tsjone ɛ in'klusa

Is it possible to add a third bed? • E' possibile aggiungere un terzo letto? • eh pos-see-bee-le ad-djun-ge-re oon tehr-tso leht-to • ɛ pos'sibile ad'dʒundʒɛre un 'tɛrtso 'lɛtto

Can you bring breakfast to the room? • Può farci portare la colazione in camera? • poo-oh far-chee por-ta-re la ko-lat-tsyo-ne een ka-me-ra • pu'ɔ 'fartʃi por'tare la kolat'tsjone in 'kamera

Where can I park the car? • Dove posso parcheggiare la macchina? • do-ve pohs-so par-ked-ja-re la mak-kee-na • 'dove 'pɔsso parked'dʒare la 'makkina

Can you make up the bill please? • Può prepararmi il conto? • poo-oh pre-pa-rar-mee eel kon-to • pu'ɔ prepa'rarmi il 'konto

Can you recommend a good hotel? • Può consigliarmi un buon hotel? • poo-oh kon-see-llyar-mee oon bwohn o-tehl • pu'ɔ konsiʎ'ʎarmi un 'bwɔn o'tɛl

Thanks for your hospitality • Grazie per la vostra ospitalità • grat-tsye per la vos-tra os-pee-ta-lee-ta • 'grattsje per la 'vostra ospitali'ta

TRAVELLING

What time does the bus leave? • A che ora parte l'autobus? • a ke o-ra par-te la-u-to-boos • a ke 'ora 'parte 'lautobus

Plane • aereo • a-eh-reo • a'ɛreo (m.s.)

Boat • nave • na-ve • 'nave (f.s.)

Train • treno • treh-no • 'trɛno (m.s.)

Ferry • traghetto • tra-get-to • tra'getto (m.s.)

The plane is delayed • l'aereo arriverà in ritardo • la-eh-reo ar-ree-ve-ra een ree-tar-do • la'ɛreo arrive'ra in ri'tardo

TRAIN

The train is cancelled • il treno è annullato • eel treh-no eh an-nool-la-to • il 'trɛno ɛ an'nullato

From what platform does the train leave for ...? • Da quale binario parte il treno per ...? • da kwa-le bee-na-ryo par-te eel treh-no per • da 'kwale bi'narjo 'parte il 'trɛno per

The train leaves from platform no.2 • il treno parte dal binario num. 2 • eel <u>treh</u>-no <u>par</u>-te dal bee-<u>na</u>-ryo <u>noo</u>-me-ro <u>doo</u>-e • il 'trɛno 'parte dal bi'narjo 'numero 'due

Where is …? • Dov'è …? • do-veh • do'vɛ

> Dining car • vagone ristorante • va-<u>go</u>-ne rees-to-<u>ran</u>-te • va'gone risto'rante (m.s.)

> Luggage car • bagagliaio • ba-ga-<u>llya</u>-yo • bagaʎ'ʎajo (m.s.)

> Sleeping car • vagone letto • va-<u>go</u>-ne <u>leht</u>-to • va'gone 'lɛtto (m.s.)

> Berths • cuccette • kut-<u>tchet</u>-te • kut'tʃette (f.p.)

Where can I buy the ticket? • Dove posso comprare il biglietto? • <u>do</u>-ve <u>pos</u>-so kom-<u>pra</u>-re eel bee-<u>llyet</u>-to • 'dove 'posso kom'prare il biʎ'ʎetto

How much does a ticket to Rome cost? • Quanto costa un biglietto per Roma? • <u>kwan</u>-to <u>kos</u>-ta oon bee-<u>llyet</u>-to per <u>ro</u>-ma • 'kwanto 'kosta un biʎ'ʎetto per 'roma

> First class • prima classe • <u>pree</u>-ma <u>klas</u>-se • 'prima 'klasse

> Second class • seconda classe • se-<u>kon</u>-da <u>klas</u>-se • se'konda 'klasse

> Single • solo andata • <u>so</u>-lo an-<u>da</u>-ta • 'solo an'data

Return • andata e ritorno • an-<u>da</u>-ta e ree-<u>tor</u>-no • an'data e ri'torno

Discounted • ridotto • ree-<u>dot</u>-to • ri'dotto

I'd like a ... seat, please • Vorrei un posto ... • <u>vor</u>-rey oon <u>pos</u>-to • vor'rɛj un 'posto

Aisle • lato corridoio • <u>la</u>-to kor-ree-<u>do</u>-yo • 'lato korri'dojo

Non-smoking • non fumatori • non foo-ma-<u>to</u>-ree • non fuma'tori

Window • lato finestrino • <u>la</u>-to fee-nes-<u>tree</u>-no • 'lato fines'trino

Is this seat free? • E' libero questo posto? • eh <u>lee</u>-be-ro <u>kwes</u>-to <u>pos</u>-to • ɛ 'libero 'kwesto 'posto

Do I have to pay a supplement? • Devo pagare un supplemento? • <u>de</u>-vo pa-<u>ga</u>-re un soop-ple-<u>men</u>-to • 'devo pa'gare un supple'mento

Has the 10:00 train already departed ? • É già partito il treno delle 10:00 ? • eh <u>dja</u> par-<u>tee</u>-to eel <u>treh</u>-no <u>del</u>-le dee-<u>eh</u>-chee ? • ɛ dʒa partito il 'trɛno delle 'djɛtʃi ?

My luggage didn't arrive • Il mio bagaglio non è arrivato • eel <u>mee</u>-o ba-<u>ga</u>-llyo non eh ar-ree-<u>va</u>-to • il 'mio ba'gaʎʎo non ɛ arri'vato

CAR

speed limit • limite di velocità • <u>lee</u>-mee-te dee ve-lo-chee-<u>ta</u> • 'limite di velotʃi'ta (m.s.)

one way • senso unico • <u>sehn</u>-so <u>oo</u>-nee-ko • 'sɛnso 'uniko (m.s.)

no parking • divieto di parcheggio • dee-vee-<u>eh</u>-to dee par-<u>ked</u>-djo • di'vjɛto di par'keddʒo (m.s.)

Where can I get a taxi ? • Dove posso prendere un taxi ? • <u>do</u>-ve <u>po</u>-sso <u>prehn</u>-de-re oon <u>ta</u>-xee ? • 'dove 'posso 'prɛndere un 'taksi ?

Can you show me the way to ...? • Può indicarmi la strada per ...? • poo-<u>oh</u> een-dee-<u>kar</u>-mee la <u>stra</u>-da per ? • pu'ɔ indi'karmi la 'strada per ?

Does this road lead to ...? • Questa strada porta a ...? • <u>kwes</u>-ta <u>stra</u>-da <u>por</u>-ta a • 'kwesta 'strada 'porta a

Can you show me on this map where I am ? • Può indicarmi sulla mappa dove mi trovo? • poo-<u>oh</u> een-dee-<u>kar</u>-mee <u>sool</u>-la <u>map</u>-pa <u>do</u>-ve mee <u>tro</u>-vo • pu'ɔ indi'karmi 'sulla 'mappa 'dove mi 'trɔvo

I would like to rent a car • Vorrei noleggiare una macchina • vor-<u>reh</u>-ee no-led-<u>dja</u>-re <u>oo</u>-na <u>mak</u>-kee-na • vor'rɛj noled'dʒare una 'makkina

51

How much is it daily for hire? • Quanto costa il noleggio al giorno? • <u>kwan</u>-to <u>kos</u>-ta eel no-<u>led</u>-djo al <u>jor</u>-no • 'kwanto 'kosta il no'leddʒo al 'dʒorno

Is tax included? • Le tasse sono comprese? • le <u>tas</u>-se <u>so</u>-no kom-<u>pre</u>-se • le 'tasse sono kom'prese

Petrol station • distributore di benzina • dees-tree-boo-<u>to</u>-re dee ben-<u>dzee</u>-na • distribu'tore di ben'dzina

Fill it up, please • Il pieno, per favore • eel <u>pyeh</u>-no per fa-<u>vo</u>-re • il 'pjɛno per favore

Unleaded petrol • benzina senza piombo • ben-<u>dzee</u>-na <u>sen</u>-tsa <u>pyom</u>-bo • ben'dzina 'sɛntsa 'pjombo

Diesel • gasolio • ga-<u>zoh</u>-lyo • ga'zɔljo (m.s.)

LPG • GPL • jeep-<u>pyehl</u>-le • gip'pjɛlle (m.s.)

Please check the tyres • Controlli le gomme per favore • kon-<u>trol</u>-lee le <u>gom</u>-me per fa-<u>vo</u>-re • kon'trolli le 'gomme per fa'vore

Can I park here? • Posso parcheggiare qui? • <u>pos</u>-so par-ked-<u>dja</u>-re <u>kwee</u> • 'posso parked'dʒare kwi

I have had an accident • Ho avuto un incidente • oh a-<u>voo</u>-to oon een-chee-<u>dehn</u>-te • ɔ a'vuto un intʃi'dɛnte

I have got a puncture • ho forato • oh fo-<u>ra</u>-to • ɔ forato

I have run out of petrol • ho terminato la benzina • oh ter-mee-<u>na</u>-to la ben-<u>dzee</u>-na • ɔ terminato la ben'dzina

The battery is flat • la batteria è scarica • la bat-te-<u>ree</u>-a eh <u>ska</u>-ree-ka • la batte'ria ɛ skarika

The car won't start • La macchina non parte • la <u>mak</u>-kee-na non <u>par</u>-te • la 'makkina non 'parte

I need a mechanic • Ho bisogno di un meccanico • oh bee-<u>zon</u>-nyo dee oon mek-<u>ka</u>-nee-ko • ɔ bi'zoɲɲo di un mek'kaniko

Can you fix it today? • La può riparare oggi? • la poo-<u>oh</u> ree-pa-<u>ra</u>-re <u>ohd</u>-djy • la pu'ɔ ripa'rare 'ɔddʒi

Borders

(formal) - Where are you from ? • Da dove viene ? • da <u>do</u>-ve <u>vye</u>-ne ? • da 'dove 'vjɛne ?

(informal) - Where are you from ? • Da dove vieni ? • da <u>do</u>-ve <u>vyeh</u>-nee ? • da 'dove 'vjɛni ?

I am from… ee io vengo da … • <u>ee</u>-o <u>ven</u>-go da … • io vengo da …

    USA • gli Stati Uniti d'America • lly <u>sta</u>-tee oo-<u>nee</u>-tee da-<u>meh</u>-ree-ka • ʎʎi 'stati u'niti da'mɛrika (m.p.)

UK • il Regno Unito • eel <u>re</u>-nyo oo-<u>nee</u>-to • il 'reɲɲo u'nito (m.s.)

Australia •l' Australia •l- a-oo-<u>stra</u>-lee-a • lau'stralja (f.s.)

New Zealand • la Nuova Zelanda • la noo-<u>oh</u>-va ze-<u>lan</u>-da • la 'nwɔva ze'landa (f.s.)

Germany • la Germania • la djer-<u>ma</u>-nee-a • la dʒer'manja (f.s.)

France • la Francia • la <u>fran</u>-cya • 'frantʃa (f.s.)

passport • passaporto • pas-sa-<u>pohr</u>-to • passa'pɔrto (m.s.)

visa • visto • <u>vee</u>-sto • 'visto (m.s.)

customs • dogana • do-<u>ga</u>-na • 'dogana (f.s.)

immigration • immigrazione • ee-mmee-gra-tsee-<u>o</u>-ne • im'migrattsjone (f.s.)

purpose of visit • scopo del viaggio • <u>skoh</u>-po del <u>vyad</u>-djyo • 'skɔpo del 'viaddʒo

I am on holiday • io sono in vacanza • <u>ee</u>-o <u>so</u>-no een va-<u>kan</u>-tsa • io 'sono in va'kanza

I am here on business • io sono qui per affari • <u>ee</u>-o <u>so</u>-no <u>kwee</u> per af-<u>fa</u>-ree • io 'sono kwi per af'fari

I am travelling...• io viaggio • <u>ee</u>-o <u>vyad</u>-djyo • io
'viaddʒo...

on my own •da solo •da <u>so</u>-lo •da 'solo

with my family • con la mia famiglia • kon la <u>mee</u>-a
fa-<u>mee</u>-llya • kon la 'mia fa'miʎʎa

in a group • in un gruppo • een oon <u>groo</u>-ppo • in
un 'gruppo

I have a … • io ho un … • <u>ee</u>-o oh oon … • io ɔ un …

work permit • permesso di lavoro • per-<u>mes</u>-so dee
la-<u>vo</u>-ro • per'messo di la'voro (m.s.)

residency permit • permesso di soggiorno • per-<u>me</u>-
sso dee sod-<u>djyor</u>-no • per'messo di sod'dʒorno
(m.s.)

study permit • permesso di studio • per-<u>me</u>-sso dee
<u>stoo</u>-dyo • per'messo di 'studjo (m.s.)

AT THE RESTAURANT

Excuse me! • Mi scusi! • mee <u>skoo</u>-zee • mi 'skuzi

Can you recommend a good …? • Potrebbe consigliarci un
buon …? • po-<u>treb</u>-be kon-see-<u>llyar</u>-tchee oon bwohn •
po'trebbe konsiʎ'ʎartʃi un 'bwɔn

Restaurant • ristorante • rees-to-<u>ran</u>-te • risto'rante (m.s.)

Café • bar • bar • bar (m.s.)

Pizzeria • pizzeria • peet-tse-<u>ree</u>-a • pittse'ria (f.s.)

Take away • take away • <u>ta</u>-ke a-<u>way</u> • 'teik a'wei (m.s.)

I would like to reserve a table • Vorrei prenotare un tavolo • vor-<u>reh-ee</u> pre-no-<u>ta</u>-re oon <u>ta</u>-volo • vor'rɛj preno'tare un 'tavolo

I would like a table for two • Vorrei un tavolo per due • vor-<u>reh</u>-ee oon <u>ta</u>-vo-lo per <u>doo</u>-e • vor'rɛj un 'tavolo per 'due

I am waiting for friends • Aspetto degli amici • as-<u>pet</u>-to <u>de</u>-lly a-<u>mee</u>-chee • as'pɛtto 'deʎʎi a'mitʃi

(formal) - What would you like? • Cosa prende? • <u>koh</u>-sa <u>prehn</u>-de • 'kɔsa 'prɛnde

(informal) - What would you like? • Cosa prendi? • <u>koh</u>-sa <u>prehn</u>-dee • 'kɔsa 'prɛndi

(formal) - Do you like ...? • Le piace/piacciono? • le <u>pja</u>-tche/ <u>pjat</u>-tcho-no • le 'pjatʃe / pjat'tʃono

(informal) - Do you like ...? • Ti piace/piacciono? • tee <u>pja</u>-tche/ <u>pjat</u>-tcho-no • ti pja'tʃe / pjat'tʃono

Do you serve breakfast / lunch / dinner ? • Servite la colazione / il pranzo / la cena ? • ser-<u>vee</u>-te la ko-la-<u>tsyo</u>-ne / eel <u>pran</u>-dzo / la <u>tche</u>-na • ser'vite la kolat'tsjone / il 'prandzo / la 'tʃena ?

Do you have vegetarian food? • Avete cibo vegetariano ? • a-<u>ve</u>-te <u>chee</u>-bo ve-je-ta-ry<u>a</u>-no ? • a'vete 'tʃibo vedʒeta'rjano ?

I don't eat pork • Io non mangio carne di maiale • <u>ee</u>-o non <u>man</u>-gyo <u>kar</u>-ne dee ma-<u>ya</u>-le • io non 'mandʒo 'karne di ma'jale

What can I get for you? • Cosa posso portarle? • <u>koh</u>-sa <u>pos</u>-so por-<u>tar</u>-le • 'kɔsa 'pɔsso por'tarle

What would you recommend? • Che cosa mi consiglia? • ke <u>koh</u>-sa mee kon-<u>see</u>-llya • ke 'kɔsa mi kon'siʎʎa

(formal) - I suggest ... • Le consiglio ... • le kon-<u>see</u>-llyo • le kon'siʎʎo

(informal) - I suggest ... • Ti consiglio ... • tee kon-<u>see</u>-llyo • ti kon'siʎʎo

Do you have a menu? • Ha un menu? • a oon me-<u>noo</u> • a un me'nu

Can you bring me the wine list? • Può portarmi la carta dei vini? • poo-<u>oh</u> por-<u>tar</u>-mee la <u>kar</u>-ta <u>de</u>-ee <u>vee</u>-nee • pu'o por'tarmi la 'karta dei 'vini

57

I'd like to drink … • Vorrei bere … • vor-<u>reh</u>-ee <u>be</u>-re • vor'rɛj 'bere

> mineral water • acqua minerale • <u>ak</u>-kwa mee-ne-<u>ra</u>-le • 'akkwa mine'rale (f.s.)

> natural water • acqua naturale • <u>ak</u>-kwa na-too-<u>ra</u>-le • 'akkwa natu'rale (f.s.)

> sparkling water • acqua frizzante • <u>ak</u>-kwa fre-<u>ddzan</u>-te • 'akkwa frid'dzante (f.s.)

> white wine • vino bianco • <u>vee</u>-no <u>byan</u>-ko • 'vino 'bjanko (m.s.)

> red wine • vino rosso • <u>vee</u>-no <u>ros</u>-so • 'vino 'rosso (m.s.)

> dry wine • vino secco • <u>vee</u>-no <u>sek</u>-ko • 'vino 'sekko (m.s.)

> sweet wine • vino dolce • <u>vee</u>-no <u>dol</u>-che • 'vino 'doltʃe (m.s.)

What do you have for dessert ? • Cosa avete come dessert ? • <u>koh</u>-sa a-<u>ve</u>-te <u>ko</u>-me de-<u>sehr</u> ? • 'kɔsa a'vete kome de'sɛr ?

How long is the wait? • Quanto si deve aspettare? • <u>kwan</u>-to see <u>de</u>-ve as-pet-<u>ta</u>-re • 'kwanto si 'deve aspet'tare

I'll have what they're having • Vorrei quello che stanno mangiando loro • vor-<u>reh</u>-ee <u>kwel</u>-lo ke <u>stan</u>-no man-<u>jan</u>-do <u>lo</u>-ro • vor'rɛj 'kwello ke 'stanno man'dʒando 'loro

What's your speciality? • Qual è la vostra specialità? • kwa-<u>leh</u> la <u>vos</u>-tra spe-cha-lee-<u>ta</u> • kwa'lɛ la 'vostra spetʃali'ta

I'd like a local speciality • Vorrei una specialità del posto • vor-<u>reh</u>-ee la spe-cha-lee-<u>ta</u> del <u>pos</u>-to • vor'rɛj la spetʃali'ta del 'posto

What are the ingredients in this dish? • Quali sono gli ingredienti in questo piatto? • <u>kwa</u>-lee <u>so</u>-no lly een-gre-<u>dyehn</u>-tee een <u>kwe</u>-sto <u>pyat</u>-to • 'kwali 'sono ʎi ingre'djɛnti in 'kwesto 'pjatto

chicken • pollo • <u>pol</u>-lo • pollo (m.s.)

beef • manzo • <u>man</u>-dzo • mandzo (m.s.)

fish • pesce • <u>pe</u>-she • 'peʃʃe (m.s.)

sausage • salsiccia • sal-<u>see</u>-chya • sal'sittʃa (f.s.)

ham • prosciutto • pro-<u>shoot</u>-to • proʃʃutto (m.s.)

cheese • formaggio • for-<u>mad</u>-djo • for'maddʒo (m.s.)

eggs • uova • oo-<u>oh</u>-va • 'wɔva (f.p.)

salad • insalata •een-sa-<u>la</u>-ta • insa'lata (f.s.)

vegetables • verdura • ver-<u>doo</u>-ra • ver'dura (f.s.)

fruit • frutta • <u>froo</u>-tta • 'frutta (f.s.)

bread • pane • <u>pa</u>-ne • 'pane (m.s.)

pasta • pasta • <u>pas</u>-ta • 'pasta (f.s.)

rice • riso • <u>ree</u>-so • 'riso (m.s.)

beans • fagioli • fa-<u>joh</u>-lee • fa'dʒɔli (m.p.)

peas • piselli • pee-<u>sehl</u>-lee • pi'sɛlli (m.p.)

May I have some … ? • Posso avere del … ? • <u>pos</u>-so a-<u>ve</u>-re del … ? • 'posso a'vere del … ?

salt • sale • <u>sa</u>-le • 'sale (m.s.)

sugar • zucchero • <u>tsook</u>-ke-ro • 'tsukkero (m.s.)

pepper • pepe • <u>pe</u>-pe • 'pepe (m.s.)

butter • burro • <u>boor</u>-ro • 'burro (m.s.)

olive oil • olio d'oliva • <u>oh</u>-lyo do-<u>lee</u>-va • 'ɔljo do'liva (m.s.)

Is the cover charge included in the bill? • Il coperto è compreso nel conto? • eel ko-<u>pehr</u>-to eh kom-<u>pre</u>-so nel <u>kon</u>-to • il ko'pɛrto ɛ kom'preso nel 'konto

Enjoy your meal • Buon appetito • boo-<u>ohn</u> ap-pe-<u>tee</u>-to • 'bwɔn appe'tito

It's my round • Offro io • <u>ohf</u>-fro <u>ee</u>-o • 'ɔffro 'io

(formal) - You can keep the change • Tenga pure il resto <u>•</u> <u>ten</u>-ga <u>poo</u>-re eel <u>reh</u>-sto • 'tɛnga pure il 'rɛsto

(informal) - You can keep the change • Puoi tenere il resto • poo-<u>oh</u>-ee te-<u>ne</u>-re eel <u>reh</u>-sto • pwɔi te'nere il 'rɛsto

Waiter! May I have …? • Cameriere! Potrei avere …? • ka-me-<u>ryeh</u>-re po-<u>treh</u>-ee a-<u>ve</u>-re • kame'rjɛre po'trɛj a'vere

Can I taste it? • Posso assaggiarlo/a? • <u>pos</u>-so as-sad-<u>djar</u>-lo • 'posso assad'dʒare

I'd like it … • Lo/a vorrei … • lo/a vor-<u>reh</u>-ee • lo/a vor'rɛj

    roast • arrosto • ar-<u>rohs</u>-to • ar'rɔsto

    baked • al forno • al <u>for</u>-no • al 'forno

    grilled • ai ferri • <u>a</u>-ee <u>fehr</u>-ree • 'ai 'fɛrri

    raw • crudo • <u>kroo</u>-do • 'krudo

    rare • al sangue • al <u>san</u>-gue • al 'sangwe

    cooked • cotto • <u>kot</u>-to • 'kɔtto

    well-done • ben cotto • behn <u>koht</u>-to • bɛn 'kɔtto

    steamed • al vapore • al va-<u>po</u>-re • al va'pore

    boiled • bollito • bol-<u>lee</u>-to • bol'lito

fried • fritto • <u>freet</u>-to • 'fritto

fresh • fresco • <u>fres</u>-ko • 'fresko

frozen • surgelato • soor-je-<u>la</u>-to • surdʒe'lato

without ... • senza ... • <u>sen</u>-tsa • 'sentsa

The check, please • il conto, per favore • eel <u>kon</u>-to per fa-<u>vo</u>-re • il 'konto per fa'vore

Do you accept credit cards? • Accettate carte di credito? • at-tchet-<u>ta</u>-te <u>kar</u>-te dee <u>kre</u>-dee-to • attʃet'tate 'karte di 'kredito

I love this dish • Mi piace molto questo piatto • mee <u>pya</u>-che <u>mol</u>-to <u>kwes</u>-to <u>pyat</u>-to • mi 'pjatʃe 'molto 'kwesto 'pjatto

I'm full • Sono sazio • <u>so</u>-no <u>sat</u>-tsyo • 'sono 'sattsjo

My compliments to the chef! • Complimenti al cuoco! • kom-plee-<u>men</u>-tee al <u>kwoh</u>-ko • kompli'menti al 'kwɔko

MONEY
How much does it cost ? • quanto costa ? • <u>kwan</u>-to <u>ko</u>-sta ? • 'kwanto 'kosta ?

Do you accept Euros/ Dollars ? • Accettate euro / dollari ? •
at-tchet-<u>ta</u>-te <u>e</u>-oo-ro / <u>dohl</u>-la-ree ? • att∫et'tate 'ɛuro /
'dollari ?

May I pay with a credit card ? • Posso pagare con carta di
credito ? • <u>pohs</u>-so pa-<u>ga</u>-re kon <u>kar</u>-ta dee <u>kre</u>-dee-to ? •
'posso pa'gare kon 'karta di 'kredito

Where's the nearest foreign exchange office ? • dove si
trova l'ufficio cambi più vicino ? • <u>do</u>-ve see <u>tro</u>-va loof-<u>fee</u>-
chyo <u>kam</u>-bee pee-<u>oo</u> vee-<u>chee</u>-no ? • 'dove si 'trova
luf'fit∫o pju vit'∫ino ?

    the bank • la banca • la <u>ban</u>-ka • la banka (f.s.)

    il cash point • il bancomat • eel <u>ban</u>-ko-mat • il
bankomat (m.s.)

I need to … • ho bisogno di … • oh bee-<u>zo</u>-nyo dee … • ɔ
bi'zoɲɲo di …

    change money • cambiare i soldi • kam-<u>bya</u>-re ee
<u>sohl</u>-dee • kam'bjare i 'sɔldi

    withdraw money • prelevare i soldi • pre-le-<u>va</u>-re ee
<u>sohl</u>-dee • prele'vare i 'sɔldi

    change a cheque • cambiare un assegno • kam-<u>bya</u>-
re oon as-<u>se</u>-nyo • kam'bjare un as'seɲɲo

get a cash advance • prelevare con carta di credito •
pre-le-<u>va</u>-re kon <u>kar</u>-ta dee <u>kre</u>-dee-to • prele'vare
kon 'karta di 'kredito

What's the commission? • qual è la commissione ? • kwal
<u>eh</u> la kom-mees-<u>syo</u>-ne ? • kwa' lɛ la kommis'sjone ?

It's free • è gratuito • eh gra-<u>too</u>-ee-to • ɛ gra'tuito

What's the exchange rate ? • qual è il tasso di cambio ? •
kwal-<u>eh</u> eel <u>tas</u>-so dee <u>kam</u>-byo ? • kwa'lɛ il 'tasso di
'kambjo ?

euros • euro • <u>eh</u>-oo-ro • ' ɛuro (m.p)

pounds • sterline • ster-<u>lee</u>-ne • ster'line (f.p.)

dollars • dollari • <u>dohl</u>-la-ree • 'dɔllari (m.p.)

SHOPS AND SERVICES

Where can I buy ...? • Dove posso comprare ...? • do-ve
<u>pohs</u>-so kom-<u>pra</u>-re • 'dove 'pɔsso kom'prare

I am looking for ... • sto cercando ... • stoh cher-<u>kan</u>-do •
stɔ tʃer'kando

a butcher shop • una macelleria • <u>oo</u>-na ma-chel-le-
<u>ree</u>-a • 'una matʃelle'ria (f.s.)

64

a bakery • un panificio • oon pa-nee-<u>fee</u>-chyo •un pani'fitʃo (m.s.)

a pastry shop • una pasticceria • <u>oo</u>-na pa-steet-tche-<u>ree</u>-a • 'una pastittʃe'ria (f.s.)

a greengrocer • un fruttivendolo • oon froot-tee-<u>ven</u>-do-lo • un frutti'vendolo (m.s.)

a supermarket • un supermercato • oon soo-per-mer-<u>ka</u>-to • un supermer'kato (m.s.)

a grocery • una drogheria • <u>oo</u>-na dro-ge-<u>ree</u>-a • una droge'ria (f.s.)

Can I try it? • Lo posso provare? • lo <u>pohs</u>-so pro-<u>va</u>-re • lo 'pɔsso pro'vare

Where's the fitting room ? • dov'è il camerino ? • do-<u>veh</u> eel ka-me-<u>ree</u>-no ? • do'vɛ il kame'rino ?

what size do you take ? • che taglia prende ? • ke <u>ta</u>-llya <u>prehn</u>-de ? • ke 'taʎʎa 'prɛnde ?

How much does it cost? • Quanto costa? • <u>kwan</u>-to <u>kos</u>-ta • 'kwanto 'kosta

It's too expensive, do you have something cheaper? • E' troppo caro, ha qualcosa di più economico? • eh <u>trohp</u>-po <u>ka</u>-ro a kwal-<u>koh</u>-sa dee pee-<u>oo</u> e-ko-<u>noh</u>-mee-ko • ɛ 'trɔppo 'karo a kwal'kɔsa di 'pju eko'nɔmiko

I can't afford this • Non posso permettermelo • non pos-so per-met-ter-me-lo • non 'pɔsso per'mettermelo

Do you have this in my size ? • Ha questo della mia misura ? • a koo-e-sto del-la mee-a mee-zoo-ra ? • a 'kwesto 'della mia mi'zura ?

I'll take it • lo prendo • lo prehn-do • lo 'prɛndo

Can you put it in a box? • Può metterlo in una scatola? • poo-oh met-ter-lo een oo-na ska-to-la • pu'ɔ met'terlo in una 'skatola

May I have a bag? • Posso avere un sacchetto ? • pos-so a-ve-re oon sak-ket-to ? • 'pɔsso a'vere un sak'ketto ?

Would you gift wrap it? • Mi fa una confezione regalo? • mee fa oo-na kon-fet-tsyo-ne re-ga-lo • mi fa una konfet'tsjone re'galo

ART

I'm interested in … art • sono interessato all'arte … • so-no een-te-res-sa-to al-lar-te … • 'sono interes'sato al'larte

classic • classica • kla-ssee-ka • 'klassika

romanesque • romana • ro-ma-na • ro'mana

gothic • gotica • go-tee-ka • 'gotika

medieval • medievale • me-dye-<u>va</u>-le • medje'vale

renaissance • rinascimentale • ree-na-shee-men-<u>ta</u>-le
• rinaʃʃimen'tale

modernist • modernista • mo-der-<u>nee</u>-sta •
modɛ'rnista

futurist • futurista • foo-too-<u>ree</u>-sta • futu'rista

contemporary • contemporanea • kon-tem-po-<u>ra</u>-ne-
a • kontempo'ranea

Where is the museum ? • Dov'è il museo ? • do-<u>veh</u> eel
moo-<u>seh</u>-o ? • do've il mu'zɛo ?

exhibition • mostra • <u>mos</u>-tra • 'mostra (f.s.)

gallery • galleria • gal-le-<u>ree</u>-a • galle'rja (f.s.)

picture gallery • pinacoteca • pee-na-ko-<u>teh</u>-ka •
pinako'tɛka (f.s.)

When's the museum open ? • quando apre il museo ? •
<u>kwan</u>-do <u>a</u>-pre eel moo-<u>zeh</u>-o ? • 'kwando 'apre il mu'zɛo ?

(formal) What kind of art are you interested in ? • che
genere di arte vi interessa ? • ke <u>je</u>-ne-re dee <u>ar</u>-te vee een-
te-<u>res</u>-sa ? • ke 'dʒɛnere di 'arte vi inte'rɛssa ?

(informal) What kind of art are you interested in ? • che genere di arte ti interessa ? • ke je-ne-re dee ar-te tee een-te-re-ssa ? • ke 'dʒɛnere di 'arte ti inte'rɛssa ?

painting • pittura • peet-too-ra • pit'tura (f.s.)

sculpture • scultura • school-too-ra • skul'tura (f.s.)

architecture • architettura • ar-kee-tet-too-ra • arkitet'tura (f.s.)

criticism • critica • cree-tee-ka • 'kritika (f.s.)

HEALTH

I need a doctor • Ho bisogno di un medico • oh bee-zon-nyo dee oon me-dee-ko • ɔ bi'zɔɲɲo di un 'mediko

Where is … ? • Dove si trova … ? • do-ve see tro-va … ? • 'dove si 'trɔ va … ?

the hospital • l'ospedale • loh-spe-da-le • lospe'dale (m.s.)

the chemist • la farmacia • la phar-ma-chee-a • la farma'tʃia (f.s.)

the dentist • il dentista • eel den-tee-sta • il den'tista (m.s.)

urgent care • la guardia medica • la <u>gwar</u>-dya <u>me</u>-dee-ka • la 'gwardja 'mɛdika (f.s.)

first aid • il pronto soccorso • eel <u>pron</u>-to sok-<u>kor</u>-so • il 'pronto sok'korso (m.s.)

Call an ambulance • Chiamate un' ambulanza • kya-<u>ma</u>-te oo-nam-boo-<u>lan</u>-tsa • kja'mate un ambu'lantsa (f.s.)

I need to be admitted to hospital • Ho bisogno di essere ricoverato all'ospedale • oh bee-<u>zon</u>-nyo dee <u>ehs</u>-se-re ree-ko-ve-<u>ra</u>-to al-lo-spe-<u>da</u>-le • ɔ bi'zɔɲɲo di 'ɛssere rikove'rato allospe'dale

I have got medical insurance • Io ho l'assicurazione medica • <u>ee</u>-o oh las-see-koo-ra-<u>tsyo</u>-ne <u>meh</u>-dee-ka • io ɔ lassikurat'tsjone 'mɛdika

I hit my head • Ho battuto la testa • oh bat-<u>too</u>-to la <u>teh</u>-sta • ɔ bat'tuto la 'tɛsta

I have lost a lot of blood • Ho perso molto sangue • oh <u>pehr</u>-so <u>mol</u>-to <u>san</u>-gwe • ɔ 'pɛrso 'molto 'sangwe

Can you give me something for the pain? • Mi può dare qualcosa per il dolore ? • mee poo-<u>oh</u> da-re koo-al-<u>koh</u>-sa per eel do-lo-re ? • mi pw' ɔ dare kwal'kɔsa per il do'lore ?

I am sick • Sono malato • <u>so</u>-no ma-<u>la</u>-to • 'sono ma'lato

I've been injured • Sono stato ferito • so-no <u>sta</u>-to fe-<u>ree</u>-to • 'sono 'stato fe'rito

I have ... • io ho ... • <u>ee</u>-o oh ... • io ɔ ...

a temperature • la febbre • la <u>fehb</u>-bre • la 'fɛbbre (f.s)

a cold • il raffreddore • eel raf-fred-<u>do</u>-re • il raffred'dore (m.s.)

a migraine • l'emicrania • le-mee-<u>kra</u>-nya • lemi'kranja (f.s.)

a cough • la tosse • la <u>tos</u>-se • la 'tosse (f.s.)

a headache • il mal di testa • eel mal dee <u>tehs</u>-ta • il mal di 'tɛsta (f.s.)

a stomachache • il mal di stomaco • eel mal dee <u>stoh</u>-ma-ko • il mal di 'stɔmako (m.s.)

a toothache • il mal di denti • eel mal dee <u>dehn</u>-tee • il mal di 'dɛnti (m.s.)

a sore throat • il mal di gola • eel mal dee <u>go</u>-la • il mal di 'gola (m.s.)

a pain in my leg • un dolore alla gamba • oon do-<u>lo</u>-re <u>al</u>-la <u>gam</u>-ba • un do'lore 'alla 'gamba (m.s.)

I am suffering from … • soffro di … • <u>sohf</u>-fro dee … • 'sɔffro di

Have you got anything for … ? • avete qualcosa contro … ? • a-<u>ve</u>-te koo-al-<u>koh</u>-sa <u>kon</u>-tro … ? • a'vete kwal'kɔsa 'kontro … ?

Can you recommend anything for … ? • può consigliarmi qualcosa contro … ? • poo-<u>oh</u> kon-see-<u>llyar</u>-mee koo-al-<u>koh</u>-sa <u>kon</u>-tro … ? • 'pwɔ konsiʎ'ʎarmi kwal'kɔsa 'kontro … ?

indigestion • l' indigestione • leen-dee-je-<u>styo</u>-ne • lindidʒes'tjone (f.s.)

diarrhoea • diarrea • la dee-a-<u>rreh</u>-a • diar'rɛa (f.s.)

travel sickness • malessere da viaggio • eel ma-<u>les</u>-se-re da vee-<u>ad</u>-djo • ma'lɛssere da 'viaddʒo (m.s.)

It's only available on prescription • è disponibile solo su riceotta • eh dee-spo-<u>nee</u>-bee-le <u>so</u>-lo soo ree-<u>cheht</u>-ta • ɛ dispo'nibile solo su ri'tʃetta

I am diabetic • sono diabetic • <u>so</u>-no dya-<u>beh</u>-tee-ko • 'sono dia'bɛtiko

I am asthmatic • sono asmatico • <u>so</u>-no az-<u>ma</u>-tee-ko • 'sono az'matiko

I am epileptic • soffro di epilessia • sof-fro dee e-pee-les-sya • 'soffro di epiles'sia

I have got my period • ho il ciclo • oh eel chee-klo • ɔ il 'tʃiklo

I am pregnant • sono incinta • so-no een-cheen-ta • 'sono in'tʃinta

I have got my contractions • ho le contrazioni •oh le kon-tra-tsyo-nee • ɔ le kontrat'tsjoni

ALLERGIES AND FOOD INTOLLERANCES

(formal) - Are you allergic to anything? • è allergico/a a qualcosa ? • eh al-lehr-gee-ko/a a kwal-koh-sa ? • ɛ al'lɛrdʒiko/a a kwal'kɔsa ?

(informal) - Are you allergic to anything? • sei allergico/a a qualcosa ? • seh-ee al-lehr-gee-ko/a a kwal-koh-sa ? • sɛi al'lɛrdʒiko/a a kwal'kɔsa ?

I am allergic to… • sono allergico a … • so-no al-lehr-gee-ko a … • 'sono al'lɛrdʒiko a …

antiobiotics • antibiotici • an-tee-byo-tee-chee • antibi'ɔtitʃi (m.p.)

pollen • polline • pohl-lee-ne • 'pɔlline (m.s.)

penicillin • penicillina • pe-nee-cheel-<u>lee</u>-na • penitʃil'lina (f.s.)

bee sting • puntura d'ape • poon-<u>too</u>-ra <u>da</u>-pe • pun'tura 'dape (f.s.)

gluten • glutine • <u>gloo</u>-tee-ne • 'glutine (m.s.)

seafood • frutti di mare • <u>froot</u>-tee dee <u>ma</u>-re • 'frutti di 'mare (m.p.)

shellfish • crostacei • kro-<u>sta</u>-che-ee • kros'tatʃej (m.p.)

Is this ...? • questo è ... ? • <u>kwe</u>-sto eh ... ? • 'kwesto ɛ ... ?

cholesterol-free • senza colesterolo • <u>sehn</u>-tsa ko-le-ste-<u>roh</u>-lo • 'sɛntsa koleste'rɔlo

gluten-free • senza glutine • <u>sehn</u>-tsa <u>gloo</u>-tee-ne • 'sɛntsa 'glutine

salt-free • senza sale • <u>sehn</u>-tsa <u>sa</u>-le • 'sɛntsa 'sale

genetically modified • geneticamente modificato • je-ne-tee-ka-<u>men</u>-te mo-dee-fee-<u>ka</u>-to • dʒenetika'mente modifi'kato low sugar • a basso contenuto di zucchero • a <u>bas</u>-so kon-te-<u>noo</u>-to dee <u>tsook</u>-ke-ro • a 'basso konte'nuto di 'tsukkero

SERVICES FOR DISABLED PEOPLE

Reserved for Disabled • Riservato ai Disabili • ree-ser-<u>va</u>-to *a*-ee dee-<u>sa</u>-bee-lee • riser'vato ai di'sabili

I am disabled • sono disabile •<u>so</u>-no dee-<u>sa</u>-bee-le •'sono di'sabile

blind • sono non vedente •<u>so</u>-no non ve-<u>dehn</u>-te • 'sono non ve'dɛnte

deaf • sono non udente •<u>so</u>-no non oo-<u>dehn</u>-te • 'sono non u'dɛnte

deaf and dumb • sordomuto • sor-do-<u>moo</u>-to • sordo'muto

(formal) - Do you have services for disabled people? • Avete servizi per i disabili ? • a-<u>ve</u>-te ser-<u>vee</u>-tsee per ee dee-<u>sa</u>-bee-lee ? • a'vete ser'vittsi per i di'sabili ?

(informal) - Do you have services for disabled people? • Hai servizi per i disabili ? • <u>a</u>-ee ser-<u>vee</u>-tsee per ee dee-<u>sa</u>-bee-lee ? • 'ai ser'vittsi per i di'sabili ?

I have got… a wheelchair • Io ho una sedia a rotelle • <u>ee</u>-o oh <u>oo</u>-na <u>seh</u>-dja a ro-<u>tehl</u>-le • io ɔ una 'sɛdja a ro'tɛlle

a hearing aid • un apparecchio acustico • oon ap-pa-<u>rek</u>-kjo a-<u>koo</u>-stee-ko • un appa'rekkjo a'kustiko

a pacemaker • un pacemaker • oon pace-<u>ma</u>-ker • un 'peɪsˌmeɪkə^r

Is/are there … • C'è / Ci sono … ? • cheh / chee <u>so</u>-no … ? • tʃɛ / tʃi 'sono … ?

toilets for the disabled • bagni per i disabili • <u>ban</u>-nyee per ee dee-<u>sa</u>-bee-lee • 'baɲɲi per i di'sabili

a access for the disabled • un accesso per i disabili • oon at-<u>tches</u>-so per ee dee-<u>sa</u>-bee-lee • un at'tʃɛsso per i di'sabili

a ramp access • una rampa di accesso • <u>oo</u>-na <u>ram</u>-pa dee at-<u>tches</u>-so • una 'rampa di at'tʃɛsso

a lift • un ascensore • oonn as-shen-<u>so</u>-re • un aʃʃen'sore

EMERGENCIES

Danger • Pericolo • pe-<u>ree</u>-ko-lo • pe'rikolo (m.s.)

Do not touch • Non toccare • non tok-<u>ka</u>-re • non tok'kare

Break glass • Rompere il vetro • <u>rom</u>-pe-re eel ve-tro • 'rompere il 'vetro

Help ! • Aiuto ! • a-y<u>oo</u>-to • a'juto

Fire ! • Al fuoco ! • al foo-<u>oh</u>-ko • al 'fwɔko

Stop ! • Stop ! • stop ! • stɔp !

Get out now ! • Uscite subito ! • oo-<u>shee</u>-te <u>soo</u>-bee-to • 'uʃite 'subito

Run ! • Scappa ! • <u>skap</u>-pa ! • 'skappa !

Call the police, please • chiama la polizia per favore • ky<u>a</u>-ma la po-lee-<u>tsee</u>-a per fa-<u>vo</u>-re • kiama la polit'tsia per fa'vore

fireman • pompiere • pom-pee-<u>eh</u>-re • pom'pjɛre

It's an emergency ! • é un' emergenza ! • eh oone-mehr-<u>jehn</u>-tsa ! • ɛ unemer'dʒɛntsa !

(formal) Could you help me please ? • Potrebbe aiutarmi ? • po-<u>treb</u>-be a-yoo-<u>tar</u>-mee ? • po'trebbe aju'tarmi ?

(informal) Could you help me please ? • Mi puoi aiutare ? • mee poo-<u>oh</u>-ee a-yoo-<u>ta</u>-re ? • mi 'pwoi aju'tare ?

Where is the ... police station ? • Dov'è la stazione di polizia ? • do-<u>veh</u> la sta-tzee-<u>o</u>-ne dee po-lee-<u>tsee</u>-a ? • dovɛ la stat'tsjone di polit'tsia ?

embassy •l' ambasciata • lam-ba-<u>sha</u>-ta • lambaʃʃata (f.s.)

consulate • il consolato • eel kon-so-<u>la</u>-to • il konso'lato (m.s.)

I have been ... • sono stato ... • <u>so</u>-no <u>sta</u>-to ... • sono stato ...

robbed • derubato • de-roo-<u>ba</u>-to • deru'bato

raped • violentato • vee-o-len-<u>ta</u>-to • violen'tato

assaulted • aggredito • ag-gre-<u>dee</u>-to • aggre'dito

I am lost • mi sono perso • mee <u>so</u>-no <u>pehr</u>-so • mi 'sono 'pɛrso

I have a flat tire • Ho una gomma a terra • oh <u>oo</u>-na go-mma a <u>teh</u>-rra • ɔ una 'gomma a 'tɛrra

COMPUTER AND INTERNET

download • scaricare • ska-ree-<u>ka</u>-re • skari'kare

online • online • on-<u>la</u>-een • on'lain

username • nome utente • <u>no</u>-me oo-<u>tehn</u>-te • nome u'tɛnte (m.s.)

website • sito web • <u>see</u>-to web • 'sito web (m.s.)

search engine • motore di ricerca • mo-<u>to</u>-re dee- ree-<u>tcher</u>-ka • mo'tore di ri'tʃerka (m.s.)

homepage • pagina iniziale • <u>pa</u>-jee-na ee-nee-<u>tsya</u>-le • 'padʒina init'tsjale (m.s.)

login • accedi • at-<u>tche</u>-dee • at'tʃɛdi

logout • esci • <u>eh</u>-schee • ɛʃi

email • email • ee-<u>meh</u>-eel • imɛil (f.s.)

Where's the nearest internet café ? • Dove si trova l'internet café ? • <u>do</u>-ve see <u>tro</u>-va <u>leen</u>-ter-net <u>ka</u>-feh ? • dove si trova lıntənet kafɛ ?

Is there wi-fi here ? • c'è il wi-fi qui ? • cheh eel wi-<u>fi kwee</u> ? • tʃɛ il wai fai kwi ?

I need a connection to internet • Ho bisogno di una connessione a internet • oh bee-<u>zo</u>-nyo dee <u>oo</u>-na kon-nes-<u>syo</u>-ne a <u>een</u>-ter-net • ɔ bi'zoɲɲo di una konnes'sjone a 'ıntənet

(formal) Can you help me with my computer ? • mi potrebbe aiutare col mio computer ? • mee po-<u>treb</u>-be a-ee-oo-<u>ta</u>-re kol <u>mee</u>-o kom-<u>pu</u>-ter ? • mi po'trebbe aju'tare kol mio kəm'pjuːtəʳ ?

(informal) Can you help me with my computer ? • mi puoi aiutare col mio computer ? • mee poo-<u>oh</u>-ee a-ee-oo-<u>ta</u>-re kol <u>mee</u>-o kom-<u>pu</u>-ter ? • mi pwoi aju'tare kol mio kəm'pjuːtə^r ?

It's crashed • si è bloccato • see eh blok-<u>ka</u>-to • si ɛ blok'kato

SPECIAL THANKS

I would like to give special thanks to all the readers from around the globe who chose to share their kind and encouraging words with me.

Knowing even just one person found this book helpful means the world to me.

If you've benefited from this book at all, I would be honored to have you share your thoughts on it, so that others would get something valuable out of this book as well.

Your reviews are the fuel for my teaching soul, and I'd be **forever grateful** to see *your* review, too.

Thank you all.

Printed in Great Britain
by Amazon